COLORADO

The Centennial State

Derek Miller, Linda Jacobs Altman,
and Stephanie Fitzgerald

Cavendish
Square
New York

Published in 2019 by Cavendish Square Publishing, LLC
243 5th Avenue, Suite 136, New York, NY 10016
Copyright © 2019 by Cavendish Square Publishing, LLC

Library of Congress Cataloging-in-Publication Data

Names: Miller, Derek, author. | Altman, Linda Jacobs, 1943- author. | Fitzgerald, Stephanie, author.
Title: Colorado / Derek Miller, Linda Jacobs Altman, and Stephanie Fitzgerald.
Description: New York : Cavendish Square, 2019 | Series: It's my state! (fourth edition) |
Includes bibliographical references and index. | Audience: Grades 3-5.
Identifiers: LCCN 2017048042 | ISBN 9781502626233 (library bound) | ISBN 9781502626134 (ebook) |
ISBN 9781502644404 (pbk.)
Subjects: LCSH: Colorado--Juvenile literature.
Classification: LCC F776.3 .M57 2019 | DDC 978.8--dc23
LC record available at https://lccn.loc.gov/2017048042

Editorial Director: David McNamara
Editor: Caitlyn Miller
Copy Editor: Nathan Heidelberger
Associate Art Director: Alan Sliwinski
Designer: Jessica Nevins
Production Coordinator: Karol Szymczuk
Photo Research: J8 Media

It's My State!

Table of Contents

SNAPSHOT
COLORADO

The
Centennial
State

Statehood

August 1, 1876

Population

5,607,154
(2017 census estimate)

Capital

Denver

State Flag

The current state flag was adopted in 1911. It is made of three stripes. Two stripes are blue and one is white. The blue represents the sky, while the white represents snow-capped mountains. In the middle left of the flag there is a red, circular "C" with a golden circle at its center. The golden disc symbolizes the sun. The red of the "C" matches the reddish ground of the state.

State Seal

Colorado's seal is a circle that is 2.5 inches (6.4 centimeters) in diameter. At the top is the so-called eye of God—an eye in a triangle. The same symbol appears on the one-dollar bill. Under the eye is the Roman fasces—an ax surrounded by a bundle of sticks. The ax symbolizes power. The sticks represent the strength of unity. Beneath the fasces is a shield with cloud-topped mountains. There is also a mining pick and hammer. At the bottom is the Latin phrase *nil sine numine*. It means "nothing without the Deity [God]" or "nothing without providence."

HISTORICAL EVENTS TIMELINE

1541

Spanish explorers reach Colorado.

Early 1800s

The Cheyenne and Arapaho arrive in Colorado after being driven out of their ancestral homelands in the east by the arrival of the Europeans.

1858

The Pikes Peak gold rush begins, drawing a hundred thousand people to Colorado.

Where the Columbines Grow

"Where the Columbines Grow" was adopted as the state song in 1915. It praises the natural beauty of the state. In 2007, the state adopted a second state song without replacing the first one. This song is John Denver's "Rocky Mountain High." It also celebrates the natural beauty of the state, in more modern terms.

State Tree

Blue Spruce

The Colorado blue spruce is the state tree. It is an evergreen with magnificent silver-blue needles. Colorado blue spruces can grow over 100 feet (30 meters) tall. Some have lived to be more than six hundred years old. Appearing only at high elevations, the tree grows alone or in small groves. The blue spruce is commonly planted around the country as an ornamental tree. It is also used as a Christmas tree due to its beautiful appearance.

1862

The first oil well is drilled in Colorado.

1876

Colorado is the thirty-eighth state admitted to the United States.

1893

Women are given the right to vote in Colorado. It is the first time this happens through a popular vote (by the state's men).

Columbine

The state flower of Colorado is the white and lavender columbine. It is also known as the Rocky Mountain columbine. This flower only grows in small areas of the Rocky Mountains in northern Colorado. It is known for its delicate beauty and rarity.

State Gemstone

Aquamarine

1960	1993	1995
The Denver Broncos play their first game.	The state gets a Major League Baseball team, the Colorado Rockies.	Denver International Airport opens. By 2017, it is the fifth-busiest airport in the country and the twentieth-busiest airport in the world.

State Insect

Colorado Hairstreak Butterfly

State Animal

Rocky Mountain Bighorn Sheep

CURRENT EVENTS TIMELINE

2012

Colorado and Washington become the first two states in America to legalize the recreational use of cannabis.

2016

The Denver Broncos win Super Bowl 50 against the Carolina Panthers.

2017

A construction crew discovers torosaurus fossils in Thornton, Colorado.

The Flatirons are tall rock formations. They are one of Boulder's most recognizable landmarks.

1 Geography

Colorado is a state of stunning natural beauty. The Rocky Mountains tower above many cities in the state. Their majesty is what many visitors think of when they imagine Colorado. But the state is also home to part of the Great Plains—a vast expanse of grassland. As a result, the geography of the state is very diverse.

The state is commonly divided into four geographical regions: the Eastern Plains, the Front Range, the Rocky Mountains, and the Colorado **Plateau**. Each of these regions is unique. The climate in each of them, as well as the animal and plant life, is very different.

The Eastern Plains

The Eastern Plains of Colorado are part of the Great Plains region of the central United States. This vast grassland prairie is flat and dry. It is subject to howling winds and long periods of drought, or lack of water. The land is used for farming and raising livestock.

Rainfall averages 15 to 20 inches (38 to 51 cm) per year, but it comes in spurts. Weeks

FAST FACT
Colorado is sometimes called the highest state in the country. It has the highest average elevation of any state (6,800 feet or 2,070 meters). It also has the highest low point of any state at 3,315 feet (1,010 m). However, the highest point in the United States is in Alaska.

The Eastern Plains are known for their farms.

of dryness can be followed by days of rain and hail. Eastern Colorado farmers use both irrigation and dryland farming methods to make their land productive.

Like most farming areas, eastern Colorado is not heavily populated. It is a place of farms and small towns with very few people per square mile. However, this is beginning to change gradually as the population of Denver increases. Some parts of the Eastern Plains are becoming "bedroom communities" for Denver. This is a term for places where people sleep before commuting to work.

The Front Range

The Front Range stands between the Eastern Plains and the western mountains. It is about 50 miles (80 kilometers) wide and 275 miles (445 km) long. Its elevation ranges from 4,921 to 14,278 feet (1,500 to 4,350 meters) above sea level. The terrain is rugged, with many different landforms. There are cone-shaped "tepee buttes" and **mesas** with flat tops and steep sides. The mysterious and beautiful Garden of the Gods is located just west of Colorado Springs. Still farther west, on the edge of the Front Range of the Rocky Mountains, lies Pikes Peak.

Colorado borders Wyoming, Nebraska, Kansas, Oklahoma, New Mexico, and Utah. Its southwest corner also touches a corner of the state of Arizona.

The red sandstone formations in the Garden of the Gods were formed by **erosion**. Over time, wind and water carved the soft stone into fantastic shapes that look like ordinary objects. Famous landmarks include the Kissing Camels, Balanced Rock, and Sleeping Giant. When two **surveyors** came upon the area in 1859, they were struck by its beauty. One

of them mentioned that it was "a fit place for the gods to assemble." The man, Rufus Cable, named the spot Garden of the Gods.

Two formations at the entry to the garden frame a large purple mountain in the distance. That is Pikes Peak, standing like a guard at the edge of the Rocky Mountains. At 14,115 feet (4,302 m) above sea level, Pikes Peak is the thirty-first-highest peak in Colorado. It is the most visited mountain in North America. Two hundred years ago, **prospectors** in their wagon trains saw it and knew they had reached their goal.

Today, the Garden of the Gods is a National Natural Landmark.

Pikes Peak was named for Zebulon Pike. In 1806, he was the first American explorer to see it. However, he never reached the top. He set out to climb the peak but was forced back by a blizzard. Edwin James made the first successful climb in recorded history in 1820. Many pioneers never made it beyond Pikes Peak and into the Rockies. They settled in the Front Range instead, drawn by the cool climate, fresh mountain air, and beautiful surroundings.

Today, about 82 percent of Colorado's people live in this region. The state's largest cities—Denver, Colorado Springs, Aurora, and Fort Collins—are there. Denver, the state capital, is the largest city in Colorado. It is nicknamed the "Mile-High City" because its elevation is 5,280 feet (1,610 m)—exactly one mile above sea level.

FAST FACT

Colorado is the eighth-largest state at 104,094 square miles (269,602 square kilometers). It is only the twenty-first most populous state, though. Its vast plains and high mountains are home to few people. Most Coloradans live just east of the Rockies, in the shadows of the Front Range.

The Rocky Mountains

The Rocky Mountains are called the backbone of North America because the Continental

Colorado's Biggest Cities

(Population numbers are from the US Census Bureau's 2017 projections for incorporated cities.)

Denver

Colorado Springs

1. Denver: population 704,621

Denver is the state capital. It began as a mining town but quickly grew in size. Today, it is a bustling city with many museums, music venues, and outdoor activities.

2. Colorado Springs: population 464,474

Located south of Denver, Colorado Springs is Colorado's largest city by area at 194.7 square miles (504 sq km). The city was named the number-one best big city by *Money* magazine in 2006, and placed first on *Outside* magazine's list of America's best cities in 2009.

3. Aurora: population 366,623

Aurora, located just outside Denver, has more than one hundred parks, seven golf courses, 6,000 acres (2,428 hectares) of open space, and 50 miles (80 km) of hiking trails. There are also twenty-seven historic landmarks.

4. Fort Collins: population 165,080

Fort Collins, in northern Colorado, was named America's best place to live in 2006 by *Money* magazine and number six in 2010. Fort Collins is also one of the towns that inspired the design of Main Street, USA, one of the areas inside Disneyland and Disney World.

5. Lakewood: population 154,958

Lakewood, southwest of Denver, has some of the best views of the Rocky Mountains. Known more as a **suburb**, Lakewood is slowly emerging as its own city with its own identity. A downtown area, Belmar, attracts people to its shopping, dining, and music.

6. Thornton: population 136,978

Located north of Denver, Thornton is also known as a suburb of the major city. Thornton has plenty to do, though. With around eighty parks and 80 miles (130 km) of trails, residents and visitors enjoy the outdoors at home and in the nearby Rocky Mountains.

7. Arvada: population 118,807

Established in 1870, the city of Arvada has tree-lined streets, parks, trails, theater, art, and diverse businesses. Its downtown neighborhood is on the National Register of Historic Places.

8. Westminster: population 112,812

When gold was discovered nearby, settlers made their homes in the area during the 1850s. The town, once called Harris, was renamed Westminster, after Westminster University, in 1911. Today, the area is known for its recreational activities, such as hiking and golf.

Fort Collins

9. Pueblo: population 111,127

Pueblo is nicknamed "Steel City" because it is one of the largest steel-producing cities in America. Pueblo is home to the Colorado State Fair. It has a large Hispanic, Italian, and Slovenian population.

Pueblo

10. Centennial: population 110,250

This city, located outside of Denver, was named Centennial in honor of Colorado's admission to the Union in 1876. It was the nation's centennial year, or one hundred years after the signing of the Declaration of Independence. Today, it is a quiet suburb and is considered one of the safest cities in the state.

Mount Elbert is the tallest mountain in the Rockies.

Divide runs through them. Rivers east of the divide flow toward the Atlantic Ocean and the Gulf of Mexico. Rivers to the west of the divide flow toward the Pacific. The Rockies are not a single mountain range but a group of more than one hundred individual ranges. They run approximately 3,000 miles (4,800 km). The Rockies stretch from northern Alberta, Canada, all the way down into New Mexico.

The Colorado Rockies are grouped into two large "belts" running north and south through the center of the state. The belts are separated by a series of high mountain valleys. At least one thousand peaks in the Colorado Rockies are more than 10,000 feet (3,050 m) above sea level. Fifty-three are over 14,000 feet (4,270 m) high. Almost no one lives in the upper reaches of those fifty-three mountains. Even the bighorn sheep leave in winter, seeking lower—and warmer—territory.

The Rockies are sparsely populated, averaging only two people per square mile (2.59 sq km). The population is concentrated in the high mountain valleys, where level ground makes farming and ranching possible. There are no major cities in the Colorado Rockies, but there are many thriving small towns.

Two of Colorado's best-known mountain towns are Aspen and Leadville. Both began as silver mining towns and were almost destroyed when the mining boom ended. However, both survived, and they have grown into very popular resort towns.

The Colorado Plateau

The Colorado Plateau is a truly western landscape. It is a place of mountains and mesas, valleys and canyons. Along the western slope of the Rockies are woodlands of juniper and piñon pine. Farther west, trees give way to semidesert shrub lands.

Like the high mountains and the Eastern Plains,

The Four Corners National Monument is at the junction of Colorado, Arizona, Utah, and New Mexico.

western Colorado is thinly populated. Its largest city is Grand Junction, with about sixty-two thousand people. Orchards and vineyards dominate the landscape around Grand Junction. With irrigation, western Colorado provides ideal conditions for wine grapes. Peaches, cherries, and nectarines are also grown there.

Three famous sites in western Colorado are Mesa Verde National Park, Four Corners National Monument, and Dinosaur National Monument. At Mesa Verde—Spanish for "green table"—ancient cliff dwellings seem to grow out of the rock. The structures were created by a people known today as the Ancestral Pueblo people. The park has more than four thousand **archaeological sites** containing the remains of ancient human habitation. The remains date back to 600 CE.

The Four Corners National Monument is the only place in the country where a person can be in four different states at the same time. The monument is located on the Navajo Reservation at the point where Arizona, Colorado, New Mexico, and Utah meet. This point is called a quadripoint.

Dinosaur National Monument is one of the largest dinosaur fossil sites in the world. Earl

In 2016, more than three hundred thousand people visited Dinosaur National Monument.

Douglass, a paleontologist (a scientist who studies prehistoric life), found the quarry in 1909. Over the years, the quarry has yielded thousands of bones, including many nearly complete skeletons. The site also contains rock art made by the Fremont people who lived in the area 800 to 1,200 years ago.

Bodies of Water

The biggest lakes in Colorado are reservoirs, which were created by damming the flow of mountain streams. Blue Mesa Reservoir is the largest of these artificial lakes. It is about 20 miles (32 km) long and features a 96-mile (154 km) shoreline. There are also dozens of natural lakes in the mountains. The largest of them, Grand Lake, covers about 1 square mile (2.6 sq km). The Ute tribe named it Spirit Lake because they believed the souls of those who had died lived in the lake's cold waters.

Colorado is the birthplace of four major rivers. The Colorado River begins west of the Continental Divide. It flows southwest for 1,470 miles (2,370 km) to the Gulf of California. The Rio Grande is located east of the Continental Divide, as are the South Platte River, which flows into the Missouri, and the Arkansas River, which flows into the Mississippi.

The Colorado River is sometimes called the "Lifeline of the Southwest."

Weather and Climate

On Colorado's Eastern Plains, summers are hot, winters are cold, and rainfall is scarce. In central and western Colorado, **altitude** determines the type of weather and average temperature. For example, the winter temperature in the high mountain city of Leadville averages 24 degrees

Fahrenheit (–4 degrees Celsius). The plains town of Colorado Springs averages about 31°F (–0.6°C). In July, differences are even more pronounced, with Leadville averaging 53°F (12°C) and Colorado Springs 68°F (20°C).

Annual snowfall also shows how climate is related to elevation in Colorado. Leadville can receive more than 200 inches (508 cm) of snow a year. Colorado Springs gets around 42 inches (107 cm). A Rocky Mountain blizzard is something to behold. For example, in 1990, a single storm dropped 50 inches (127 cm) of snow at Echo Lake in north-central Colorado. Wind-driven snow brought traffic to a stop on the highway between Boulder and Denver.

One of Colorado's strangest weather patterns is the chinook wind. A chinook wind is warm and dry, swooping down from the mountains at near-hurricane speeds. One can raise the temperature 40 or 50°F (22.2 to 27.8°C) in an hour's time.

Denverites dig out after a 2016 snowstorm.

Colorado's Animals

From the plains to the plateau, Colorado's wildlife is varied and interesting. The Eastern Plains have small mammals such as rabbits, prairie dogs, skunks, and ground squirrels, along with the coyotes that feed on them.

Wherever there are prairie dogs, there will be burrowing owls. These small brown owls live in abandoned prairie dog burrows. Burrowing owls are on Colorado's list of threatened species. Their habitat is shrinking, partly because development is destroying prairie dog towns. Colorado's Partners in Flight program has created a conservation plan. It includes protecting burrows and reducing the use of insecticides, especially during the owls' breeding season.

Colorado's mountains are home to elk, moose, and bighorn sheep. Foxes, badgers, and beavers

FAST FACT
Colorado has always been well known for its climate. In 1900, an estimated one-third of the people living in the state were there just for that reason. The state's fresh mountain air and sunshine were said to be good for people with a lung disease called tuberculosis.

Mapping Colorado

When eastern Colorado became part of the United States in 1803, the region was mostly unmapped. The following year, Lewis and Clark led their famous expedition across the United States. They went far north of Colorado, but their discoveries began to shed light on the vast western expanse that the United States now owned.

In 1806, the first official American expedition entered modern-day Colorado. It was led by a US Army lieutenant by the name of Zebulon Pike. Pike discovered what would later be named Pikes Peak. He also explored and mapped a large area of the region. However, he eventually crossed into Spanish territory in what is now southern Colorado. He and his men were captured and questioned before being escorted out of Spanish territory.

His expedition was a vital source of early information about modern-day Colorado. He wrote a book about his journey that was quite

Pikes Peak

popular at the time. In it, he describes the majestic beauty of the area and its mountains. He also records what happened when he tried to **summit** Pikes Peak:

> Here we found the snow middle deep; no sign of beast or bird inhabiting this region. The thermometer which stood at 9° above 0 [−12.8 degrees Celsius] at the foot of the mountain, here fell to 4° below 0 [−20°C]. The summit of the Grand Peak, which was entirely bare of vegetation and covered with snow, now appeared at the distance of 15 or 16 miles [24.1 to 25.7 km] from us, and as high again as what we had ascended, and would have taken a whole day's march to have arrived at its base, when I believed no human being could have ascended to its [pinnacle].

Pike was forced to turn back. It was not until 1820 that the mountain was summited for the first time in recorded history.

The difficulty of mapping Colorado did not end with Pike's expedition. In the 1860s and 1870s, surveyors were sent to Colorado Territory to establish its boundaries. The surveyors attempted to create boundaries that were straight lines. If you look at a map of Colorado, it appears to be a rectangle. However, the surveyors struggled to get it right. Pressed for time, they sometimes created borders that zigged and zagged. They placed markers in this fashion, even though the borders were supposed to be straight.

When Colorado became a state, treaties and American laws made these markers the state border. If you look at detailed maps of the state, you can see that it is not truly a rectangle. There are several places where the surveyors got off track and were forced to correct their course. Their mistakes live on in the modern boundaries of the state.

Burrowing owls' eggs hatch in the summer.

also thrive in the region. Bears may also be found, but only a few of these creatures live year-round at the highest altitudes. Like the bighorn sheep, some of these bears move to lower altitudes for winter.

The animals of western Colorado have at least one trait in common. All can survive in a land of little rainfall. Porcupines, weasels, hares, and mule deer live where the juniper and piñon pine give way to sand and sagebrush. Predators that hunt these animals include coyotes, bobcats, and mountain lions. Golden eagles may also be found in this area.

Protecting the Environment

As the population of Colorado continues to grow, many issues face the state's plants, animals, and people. Air and water pollution are on the rise as cities expand. Climate change threatens the state's delicate ecosystems. Water itself is becoming a scarce resource in the state. The Colorado River, which runs from Colorado through six other states, is in danger of running out of water. Luckily, Coloradans have united to protect their state's natural resources. In 2015, the state of Colorado adopted a climate plan to try to minimize the impact of climate change.

Rocky Mountain National Park and Other Top Attractions

In 1915, President Woodrow Wilson created America's tenth national park: Rocky Mountain National Park. Today, the park spans more than 400 square miles (1,036 square kilometers) near the town of Estes Park. Visitors to Rocky Mountain National Park enjoy hiking, scenic drives, winter activities like snowshoeing and sledding, and summer activities like camping. In 2016, Rocky Mountain National Park hosted 4.5 million people. In fact, it is one of America's most popular national parks. Only three national parks receive more visitors than Rocky Mountain National Park.

It's no surprise that visitors flock to the Rockies and Colorado's other mountain ranges. Colorado is a first-class climbing destination. Climbers from all over come to the state to tackle tall peaks and soak in the state's beauty. The height of Colorado's mountains is one reason that it's a favorite climbing spot. Mountains that are more than 14,000 feet (4,267 m) tall are called fourteeners. Colorado has an astonishing fifty-three peaks that are classified as fourteeners. While fourteeners can be found throughout Colorado, one of the most well-known is located in Rocky Mountain National Park: Longs Peak.

Aside from fourteeners and Rocky Mountain National Park, Colorado offers other notable outdoor attractions like Mesa Verde National Park, Garden of the Gods National Natural Landmark, and Colorado National Monument.

Visitors take advantage of Rocky Mountain National Park's trails.

What Lives in Colorado?

Flora

Rocky Mountain Juniper This medium-sized tree typically grows up to 33 to 66 feet (10 to 20 m) tall. In Colorado, it typically grows at elevations of 5,000 to 7,500 feet (1,525 to 2,285 m). While the tree technically has cones, they look like blue berries. Native Americans have been using the berries to make traditional medicine for generations.

Quaking Aspen These trees have bright white bark and leaves that turn to vibrant colors in the fall. They are named because of their broad leaves that quake—or shake—in even a light breeze. One interesting fact about aspens is that a single root system can send up multiple trees. The trees themselves have short lifespans of less than 150 years. But the root system can live much longer. The oldest known living organism on the planet is a quaking aspen root system in Utah that is around eighty thousand years old.

Bristlecone pine

Plains Cottonwood The plains cottonwood is a large tree that can grow up to 190 feet (58 m) tall. It grows across a huge area of the United States but only in the east of Colorado. It is the state tree of Wyoming, Nebraska, and Kansas.

Piñon Pine The piñon pine grows scattered across Colorado's low mountains and in other southwestern states. Its cones contain edible seeds known as pinyon nuts or pine nuts. They are a common snack food and can be found in grocery stores across the country.

Bristlecone Pine The bristlecone pine can be found at the highest elevation of any tree in Colorado—up to nearly 12,000 feet (3,660 m). This is known as the tree line. Above this point, trees cannot grow and the landscape is barren and rocky. These trees are often twisted and gnarled due to the high winds of the mountains they grow on.

Fauna

Black Bear Black bears are found throughout western Colorado. They are a common sight on trails and even in some towns and cities—where they raid dumpsters looking for food. Males average 275 pounds (125 kilograms), while females typically weigh around 175 pounds (80 kg). Despite their size, bears usually run away from humans when they encounter them in the wild.

Rocky Mountain bighorn sheep

Rocky Mountain Bighorn Sheep These wild sheep can grow to weigh up to 300 pounds (136 kg). Their horns alone can weigh up to 31 pounds (14 kg). They live in mountainous terrain where their hooves are suited to walking along narrow rock shelves and over jagged rocks. The sheep live in groups with members of the same sex.

Lynx The lynx is a wild cat that weighs between 20 and 30 pounds (9.1 and 13.6 kg) as an adult. They have gray fur that is spotted and long tufts of black hair on top of their ears. Around 1973, lynx were completely driven out of Colorado, but they were reintroduced to the state in 1999. Today, there are a couple hundred lynx in Colorado.

Bobcat

Bobcat Bobcats are slightly smaller than lynx. However, the two animals are similar in appearance and are often confused for each other. One way to tell the two apart is that lynx have much longer ear tufts. Bobcats tend to prey on rabbits, which they ambush rather than chase.

Mountain Lion Mountain lions are much larger than lynx and bobcats. Males average 150 pounds (68 kg). Females average 90 pounds (40 kg). Their preferred prey is deer, but they also hunt smaller prey as well as livestock. Mountain lions are also known as cougars, pumas, and sometimes panthers in the western United States.

Mountain lion

The Cliff Palace at Mesa Verde National Park was constructed by the Ancestral Pueblo.

2 The History of Colorado

Colorado has a long, exciting history. Early on, it was home to many Native American people. Some of them built the majestic cliff dwellings that still draw visitors to this day. After the arrival of Europeans, the state was at the center of the "Wild West" mythology. People from around the country came to the state to be mountain men or look for gold.

The First People

Colorado's first people, known as Paleo-Indians, arrived about thirteen thousand years ago. They hunted mastodons, mammoths, and other gigantic creatures. When big game became scarce, the Paleo-Indians turned to hunting smaller game. They also began gathering plant matter to supplement their diets.

The descendants of these early people were also hunter-gatherers. The descendants used to be called Anasazi, which is a Navajo word

This example of Puebloan pottery is part of the Heard Museum's collection.

meaning "enemies of our ancestors." Today, the preferred term is Ancestral Pueblo people. Scholars refer to the Ancestral Pueblo people living from 500 BCE to about 800 CE as Basket Makers because they made beautiful baskets that had many uses. The next phase of the people's history, 800 CE until about 1300 CE, is known as the Puebloan era. During this time, the Ancestral Pueblo people built magnificent homes into the cliff faces of southwestern Colorado and farmed the land above. Some of these homes are still standing today. They lived undisturbed by outsiders until the first Spanish explorers arrived in the late sixteenth century. (Other Native peoples, including the Ute, Comanche, Cheyenne, Arapaho, and Kiowa, made their homes in what is now Colorado in the 1700s and the 1800s.)

Spanish explorers were followed in time by settlers, who came for the land, and fortune seekers, who came for the silver and gold. All played a part in the history of the Centennial State.

Baskets made by the Ancestral Pueblo are celebrated for their beauty.

The Ancestral Pueblo People

The Ancestral Pueblo people have long been a mystery to archaeologists. Exactly who were they? How did they learn to build magnificent, multistory "apartment houses"? Why did they suddenly abandon it all and seemingly disappear? Nobody knows all the answers to these questions. What scientists and historians do know is that the Ancestral Pueblo people were hunters and gatherers. They also made pottery and developed farming techniques. The Ancestral Pueblo people built their homes using sandstone rocks held together with adobe (sun-dried clay and straw). Many of these homes are extraordinary cliff dwellings. The remains of these magnificent

American bison attracted Native peoples to Colorado.

structures can still be seen in Mesa Verde National Park.

No one knows for certain why the Ancestral Pueblo people seem to have disappeared. Some scholars blame a long drought that destroyed their crops. Many think that the Ancestral Pueblo people migrated out of the area to join other Native cultures. The Pueblo, a Native American group found in the Southwest, are the descendants of the Ancestral Pueblo people.

Long after the Ancestral Pueblo people were gone, other Native American peoples continued to settle in what is now Colorado. These included the Cheyenne, Kiowa, Arapaho, Comanche, and Ute. Most of these Natives were hunters and gatherers. They often followed the bison herds on the Eastern Plains, bringing along their homes and families.

The Ute favored higher altitudes. Some of them lived 10,000 feet (3,050 m) above sea level. For food, they gathered wild plants and fished in the rivers and streams. They also hunted elk and deer, using the meat for food and using the hides for their homes and clothing. Later, the Ute traded the hides and other goods for horses and other necessities. The Ute were skilled riders and used horses for hunting. But life for all the Native American groups in the region began to change as European explorers and settlers arrived in greater numbers.

The First Europeans Arrive

In 1682, a French explorer named René-Robert Cavelier, sieur de La Salle, claimed a huge area

Native Americans in Colorado

Today, the Ute are the oldest Native tribe originally from Colorado. The Ancestral Pueblo people who built the cliff dwellings in the southwest corner of the state had left the area by around 1300 CE. Migration added the Apache, Arapaho, Comanche, Cheyenne, Shoshone, and Pueblo tribes to the state.

The Pueblo tribes lived in villages in homes made of mud. They grew corn, beans, peppers, and other vegetables. The other tribes lived on the Great Plains and were more **nomadic**. Their homes were either wickiups or tepees. Wickiups were wood framed and covered with brush and could be made in a few hours. The tepees were conical, with wood poles meeting at the top, and were covered with bison skins. The women built the homes. Women were also responsible for dragging the frames when the tribe moved. The men were primarily hunters, seeking bison, deer, antelope, and small game. The Plains tribes originally used dogs to pull their belongings when they moved, but when the Spanish brought horses to North America, they became skilled riders.

Members of the Ute tribe in 1880

Spotlight on the Arapaho

The Arapaho is a tribe that lived in the plains region of Colorado. After gold was discovered near Denver in 1858, confrontations between the tribe and white settlers intensified. A treaty in 1861 attempted to remove the southern branch of the tribe. However, it was never ratified (approved).

Food: The Arapaho diet consisted of mostly meat that they hunted, such as bison, deer, and elk. The tribe also gathered food such as berries, vegetables, and roots. Hunting not only provided food, but it provided materials for shelter, clothing, and trading.

Clothing: Arapaho women wore leggings and dresses. They used paint, porcupine quills, elk teeth, and beads for decoration. Arapaho men wore breechcloths, or loincloths, shirts (sometimes), leggings, and moccasins.

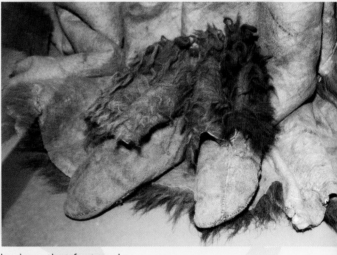

Warm moccasins helped the Arapaho endure cold winters.

Powwows: Powwows, which began in the mid-1800s, were social gatherings that featured competitive dancing and honoring ceremonies. Powwows still happen around the country today.

Sun Dance: The Sun Dance is a ceremony during which the Arapaho pray to their higher powers. It generally takes place during the summer, and it lasts around seven days. The last four days involve the dancing. It was, and still is, one of the tribe's most sacred ceremonies.

René-Robert Cavelier, sieur de La Salle, lived from 1643 to 1687.

of land in central North America for France. La Salle himself never visited the region that is now Colorado. He simply claimed everything between the Mississippi River and the Rocky Mountains. The territory extended northward to the present-day Canadian border and south to the Gulf of Mexico. La Salle named this vast region "Louisiana" in honor of King Louis XIV of France.

The Spanish were the first Europeans to actually explore Colorado. In 1706, Juan de Ulibarri led an expedition as far as present-day Pueblo. He promptly claimed the "new" territory for Spain.

Dispute Over Colorado

In 1803, the United States bought the whole Louisiana Territory from France for $15 million (more than $300 million in today's dollars). With one purchase—which became known as the Louisiana Purchase—President Thomas Jefferson doubled the size of the country. The next step was to explore this new addition.

That job fell, in part, to a twenty-seven-year-old army lieutenant named Zebulon Pike. In 1806, Pike set out to explore the southwestern borders of the Louisiana Purchase. It was on this trip that he discovered the peak that bears his name. Pike also had a secret mission. Spain had conquered and settled all of Mexico and most of the present-day American Southwest, including part of Colorado. The US government asked Pike to check the strength of Spanish settlements in the region. Pike investigated the situation, traveling south from Colorado to the area that now includes New Mexico. He and his men were arrested by Spanish authorities and taken to Santa Fe, New Mexico, but they were later released by the Spanish.

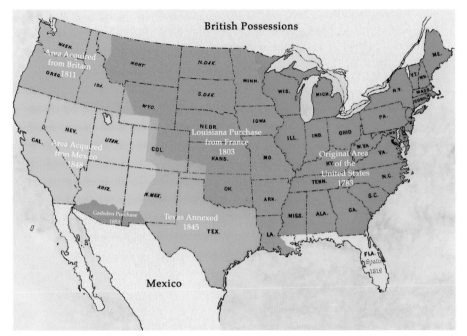

Because of the Pike incident, the United States and Spain held talks about the boundaries of the Louisiana Purchase. In 1819, a treaty between the two nations gave northern and eastern Colorado to the United States, and southern and western Colorado to Spain.

In 1821, Mexico won its independence from Spain. It acquired all the Spanish territory in what is now the United States, including parts of Colorado. The new Mexican government did not have the resources to develop this large area. It welcomed Americans into the Rocky Mountain wilderness.

This map shows how America grew over time. The territory of the Louisiana Purchase is shown in purple.

Trappers and Traders

A group of sturdy adventurers who became known as mountain men gladly accepted the invitation from Mexico. They were strong, hearty men who lived by trapping beaver and other fur-bearing animals. The pelts were sold to make clothing and other goods.

A Frederic Remington illustration of mountain men

Animal pelts were fashioned into clothing and accessories, like this beaver-fur top hat.

The mountain men came from all over the United States and Canada. Some were interested in exploring, and some just hoped to make a profit from this new land. Many of them had little or no education, but they were wise in the ways of nature. They often served as guides, trackers, and scouts.

The mountain men knew that the Native Americans still controlled the land in Colorado. For the most part, the mountain men respected the **indigenous** peoples' rights. White settlement was limited to a few trading posts or forts. Both mountain men and Native Americans traded at these outposts. One of the best-known posts was Bent's Fort in southeastern Colorado, near the present-day town of La Junta. The legendary tracker Kit Carson once worked there. His title was chief hunter, and his job was to keep the fort well supplied with meat.

In the 1840s, the world of the mountain men began to change. Because of over trapping, beaver populations had shrunk. Changes in fashion also made beaver fur less popular. Without as many beaver and with a smaller demand for the pelts, making a living as a trapper became very hard. This issue, combined with disaster and disease, caused the abandonment of Bent's Fort in 1849.

After the United States defeated Mexico in the Mexican-American War, which lasted from 1846 to 1848, Mexico gave up almost all its territory in the American Southwest to the United States for $15 million. Besides part of Colorado, the territory included all of present-day California, Nevada, and Utah, and parts of Arizona, New Mexico, and Wyoming. In 1853, an additional US purchase of almost 30,000 square miles (77,700 sq km) of land in what is now southern Arizona and New Mexico would give the continental United States (excluding Alaska) its present borders.

The Colorado Gold Rush

In January 1848, gold was discovered in California, starting one of the largest human migrations in American history. During the "gold rush," about three hundred thousand people hoping to strike it rich headed for California. Many of these people passed through Colorado on their quest for gold. In 1858, a party led by miner William Green Russell found gold at Little Dry Creek, just south of the present-day site of Denver. This brought more prospectors to the area. Russell's discovery was followed by three larger finds in Colorado in 1859. Thousands of people tacked "Pikes Peak or Bust" signs on their wagons and headed west to make their fortunes. Towns sprang up almost overnight. Montana City, Denver City, and Auraria became the core of modern Denver.

Through the next several years, miners struck gold in different parts of Colorado. In 1859, gold was found near present-day Leadville, now one of Colorado's famous mining towns. In 1875, prospectors found a large deposit of lead carbonate ore there. The ore contained large quantities of

FAST FACT
Life in Colorado was hard for prospectors— people seeking to make their fortune by finding gold. Many mining communities were tent cities with few buildings. It's no surprise that most prospectors soon returned home after a short stay in Colorado.

Important Coloradans

James P. Beckwourth

Beckwourth was born into slavery in Virginia. His master later freed him, and Beckwourth went on to become a mountain man in Colorado. He also lived with the Crow for many years and experienced Native American life firsthand. Beckwourth wrote a memoir of his experiences in the West. He was the only African American to do so.

James P. Beckwourth

Clara Brown

Born into slavery, Brown married and had four children. But her family was sold off to different owners. She was later freed and set off to look for them. Hearing rumors that her daughter was out West, she moved to Colorado. There, she became a pillar of the community and helped many African Americans make their way to the state and begin new lives there. She eventually found one of her daughters at the age of eighty.

Buffalo Bill Cody

Buffalo Bill rose to fame in the Indian Wars at a young age. He was awarded the Medal of Honor for his bravery in combat. He later started his famous Wild West show. The show traveled across the country performing acts relating to the West. Although he had few ties to the state, Bill decided he wanted to be buried in Colorado. Today, his grave is a famous tourist attraction.

Clara Brown

Ruth Handler

Handler was born in Denver in 1916 to a family of Polish Jewish immigrants. She and her husband founded a business to make dollhouse furniture. But Handler had an idea. She wanted to create a doll for little girls that was older than they were. The result was the Barbie doll. It was an instant success and became the best-selling toy in history.

Little Raven

Little Raven was a famous chief of the Southern Arapaho. He lived from around 1810 to 1889. During this time, conflict between Native Americans and white settlers in Colorado was intense. Little Raven spent his life working for peace. Even after the Sand Creek Massacre, when more than 150 Native Americans were murdered, Little Raven did not resort to violence.

Hattie McDaniel

McDaniel was born in Kansas but moved to Denver at the age of six. She entered show business in the city and performed on the local radio. She later moved to Milwaukee and then Hollywood to continue her career. She was a famous actress and appeared in many films. She became the first African American to receive an Academy Award, for her role in *Gone with the Wind*.

Buffalo Bill Cody

Bill Pickett

This famous cowboy was born to African American and Cherokee parents. While an estimated one-fourth of cowboys were black, he is the most famous. Pickett competed in rodeos and starred in Wild West shows of the time. He even invented a new rodeo event that is still done today known as steer wrestling. This is when the cowboy jumps off his horse and wrestles a steer to the ground.

Zebulon Pike

Born in 1779, Pike did more than lead the famous expedition that explored Colorado. Years later, during the War of 1812, he was promoted to the rank of brigadier general. Despite his high rank, he led the assault on York (now Toronto) from the front lines. He and his men successfully took the city, but he was mortally wounded in the battle.

Little Raven

This photograph of gold miners in Eagle River Canyon was taken in 1905.

silver. It was only the first of many silver discoveries in the area. By 1878, the city of Leadville had become one of the most important mining camps in the nation. It produced a crop of overnight millionaires.

The most famous of these mining millionaires was Horace Tabor, the "Silver King." Tabor went from storekeeper to millionaire in 1877 when he "grubstaked" two prospectors, or gave them tools and supplies in exchange for a share of anything they found at the Little Pittsburgh Mine. What they found was silver—lots of it. Tabor grubstaked several other expeditions. His fortune grew. In late 1879, he bought the Matchless Mine for $117,000 (more than $2.5 million in today's money). People thought he was crazy because the Matchless had plunged its previous owners into debt and returned nothing. But Tabor had a hunch, and he was right. By the spring of 1880, the Matchless was producing a $2,000 profit each day. That's around $40,000 a day in today's dollars! Tabor became the richest of all the silver millionaires.

The good times in Leadville ended in 1893. That's when a severe economic depression hit the country. The government stopped buying silver to make coins. The price of silver dropped. Tabor and many other miners lost nearly everything.

Horace Tabor made his fortune by investing in silver miners and buying mines.

The Colorado War

The mining boom was just under way when Colorado became a US territory. Colorado's status as a territory became official

Tectonic Plates of Playdough

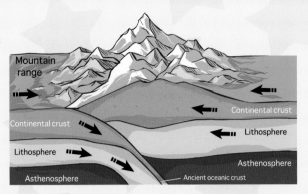

Mountain ranges are formed when Earth's plates move.

Earth's outer shell is made of a series of massive plates. These plates generate huge amounts of force, pressing and pulling against each other. This is how Earth's terrain is formed. One way that mountain ranges form is when these plates slide into each other.

You can see this for yourself by doing an experiment. First, you can make your own playdough.

Supplies

- 2 cups of white flour
- 1 cup of salt
- 1 tablespoon of oil
- 3/4 cups of water
- 2 drops of red food coloring

Instructions

1. Combine all the ingredients in a bowl.
2. Knead the playdough until it is the right consistency.
3. If your playdough is too dry, slowly add more water. If it is too wet, slowly add more flour.
4. Divide the playdough into two balls.
5. Roll and press the balls until you are left with two plates.
6. Push the plates into one another.
7. What happened? Maybe one plate went over the other. Or maybe the two plates smashed together. These are both ways that mountains can form where two tectonic plates meet. Of course, the process takes millions of years when two tectonic plates—and not playdough—are involved.

Black Kettle was a Southern Cheyenne chief who worked toward brokering peace with the United States. He was killed by US soldiers in 1868.

on February 28, 1861. The new territory immediately created a legislature, or lawmaking body, called the Territorial Assembly. At its first meeting, the assembly created seventeen counties, made plans for the University of Colorado, and chose Colorado City as the territorial capital.

The arrival of settlers became of increasing concern to Native Americans in the area. In 1851, ten years before Colorado became a territory, the United States signed the Horse Creek Treaty with the Cheyenne and other tribes. The treaty stated that prospectors and settlers would not be allowed to encroach upon the Cheyenne's traditional hunting grounds. By 1861, however, the newcomers were building houses, establishing towns, and stringing telegraph wires across the mountains and the prairies—right in the middle of the Cheyenne's land. Soldiers shot a Cheyenne chief in 1864. Native Americans responded with violence. Then, Colorado soldiers attacked and destroyed a village in Sand Creek. They murdered hundreds of Cheyenne and Arapaho people, many who were fleeing for their lives. The Sand Creek Massacre, as it was later called, led to changes in the **federal government's** Native American policies.

Fighting between settlers and Native Americans continued. The government forced many Cheyenne, Sioux, Arapaho, and Ute to move off their lands and onto reservations. Nathan C. Meeker, the federal agent in charge of the Ute reservation, tried to force the Ute to become farmers. In 1879, they rebelled, killing Meeker and others. The Meeker Massacre was the last big clash between Colorado's indigenous people and settlers. Army forces overpowered the Native Americans, who returned to the reservations.

Statehood and Growth

On August 1, 1876, Colorado became the thirty-eighth state to join the United States. The Leadville silver boom was already under way. Hopes ran high as Coloradans settled down to the business of building a state. More schools and universities were opened. Miles of new railroad tracks were laid down. Farmers developed dryland farming techniques on the plains. Dryland farming includes, among other things, planting drought-resistant crops. Another part of dryland farming involves increasing the water absorption and reducing the moisture loss from soil. By the turn of the twentieth century, Colorado had a population of 539,700 people. Mining and agriculture were important to the economy.

Colorado's mining industry survived the silver collapse of 1893, largely because of gold. A few gold strikes kept the industry going. Some mines also made money from coal and other minerals.

Farmers on the Eastern Plains used a combination of dryland farming methods and irrigation to develop the land. They produced good crops of sugar beets, as well as wheat and other grains.

When World War I (1914–1918) began, Great Britain and its allies in Europe needed raw materials. They bought food products from Colorado farms and metals such as tungsten and molybdenum from Colorado mines. When the United States entered the war in 1917, Colorado

Colorado Day

When Colorado became a state on August 1, 1876, it was just twenty-eight days after the one hundredth birthday—or centennial—of the United States. This is why the state's nickname is the Centennial State.

To mark Colorado's admission to the United States, Colorado Day is celebrated each year on August 1. Businesses and agencies around the state hold events to mark the occasion. Restaurants often offer deals to encourage people to come in. In 2017, Dunkin' Donuts gave away Colorado-themed donuts to customers.

Museums across the state often have promotions as well. Many open their doors to any resident of the state for free. History Colorado Center in Denver offered free admission in 2017. Birthday cake was sold to celebrate the day, and the governor attended the event. Many different groups provided live music, and local businesses set up tents. Local museums across the state associated with History Colorado also hosted events and offered free admission.

Eldorado Canyon State Park is just one of Colorado's forty-two state parks with free admission on Colorado Day.

On Colorado Day, state parks also waive their admission fee and are open to the public. There are forty-two state parks spread across Colorado. They host many different activities, from hiking and fishing to water sports and mountain climbing. Typically, you must buy an annual pass for the park or pay each time you go.

Because there are so many events and free admission to attractions, Colorado Day is a great day to visit the state. You can learn about its interesting history at many different museums. You can also explore its natural beauty in one of its many state parks.

farmers and miners increased production even more.

During the 1920s, Colorado built paved highways for automobile traffic and expanded its oil industry. By 1930, the state's population topped one million for the first time in history.

The US Air Force Academy is in Colorado Springs.

Also by 1930, the American stock market had collapsed, and so had the economy of the nation. This began what came to be known as the Great Depression. In Colorado, as elsewhere, many people lost their jobs, and some lost their homes. The economy did not recover until the United States entered World War II in December 1941. The US government decided that Colorado would be a safe location for military installations and other federal facilities. Soon, several government offices, defense plants, and military bases opened in the state. Many of them stayed after the war ended. So did the people who staffed them. President Dwight D. Eisenhower established the US Air Force Academy in 1954. Four years later, the Colorado Springs facility was ready to admit students. By 1960, Colorado's population had grown to more than 1.7 million. Three counties in the Front Range—Denver, Adams, and Jefferson—grew especially rapidly. The state's Eastern Plains lost people as quickly as the Front Range gained them. During the 1970s and 1980s, the suburbs around Denver became more heavily populated.

Throughout the 1980s and 1990s—and into the twenty-first century—the old standbys of mining and agriculture became less important to Colorado's economy. Old mining towns such as

Aspen is a popular town and ski resort.

Aspen and Telluride found new life as expensive ski resorts. Technological industries flourished. Tourism became an important source of income for the state.

Immigration in the Modern World

Today, Colorado remains one of the fastest-growing states in the country. Between 2015 and 2016, it had the seventh-highest population growth rate in the United States. Denver and Colorado Springs—both along the Front Range—were the cities that saw the most growth. This rapid expansion is expected to continue as Colorado draws more and more people from around the country and the globe.

Most people who move to Colorado are American citizens from other states. In 2016, most people new to the state came from California. Large numbers also moved from Texas, Florida, Illinois, and Arizona.

But there is another group of people that is also coming to Colorado looking for a new place to call home: refugees. Most refugees flee their country of birth due to violence or war. They are

unable to return home because their lives would be threatened. Common countries of origin as of 2018 include Syria, Iraq, Afghanistan, and Myanmar. Many refugees from Afghanistan and Iraq were in danger because they risked their lives to aid the US military.

Colorado has a history of welcoming refugees with open arms. In 2017, the federal government reduced the number of refugees that the United States would accept. In response, the governor of Colorado hosted an event on June 20, World Refugee Day, at the state capitol. He defended the idea that the United States should shelter refugees and give them opportunities in this country. He pointed out that refugees often become important members of the community and small business owners. In his speech, he said, "Whatever else is happening, Colorado is here for you. Colorado is going to remain a welcoming state."

Governor John Hickenlooper speaks at a World Refugee Day celebration in 2017.

Young people, like these students in Denver, make up more than 20 percent of Colorado's population.

3 Who Lives in Colorado?

Colorado is a state full of newcomers. Just 30 percent of Coloradans over the age of twenty-five were born in the state. The majority moved there later in life. As a result, the state is becoming more and more diverse. African American, Asian, and Hispanic communities, once small, are becoming larger and larger. These newcomers support Colorado's economy and are often fiercely proud of their new home.

Coloradans' Ancestry

Since its days as a US territory, Colorado has been home to a population that is largely Caucasian, or white. People of Hispanic descent have always made up the largest ethnic minority. They outnumber all other minority groups combined. The same ratio, or proportion, holds true today. Caucasians make up almost 87.5 percent of the population. Some are direct descendants of European and American explorers and settlers who came to the region hundreds of years ago. Others are from families that have lived in Colorado for the last few decades. Colorado residents may also come from different parts of the country.

FAST FACT
Colorado is home to some of the most-educated people in the country. More than 39 percent of people in the state have at least a bachelor's degree. By this standard, the only state that ranks higher is Massachusetts.

Native Americans

The people with the longest history in Colorado are today one of its smallest minority groups. Native Americans account for only 1.6 percent of the population, equal to about eighty-eight thousand people. The state is home to two Ute reservations: the Southern Ute Reservation and the Ute Mountain Reservation.

Ute dancers perform in 2002.

It can be a struggle for Native peoples to live in the modern world while still trying to hold on to their ancient traditions. Organizations such as the Southern Ute Cultural Center can help. Through its museum, the group aims to be "the principal conservator and interpreter of our Tribe's history, our stories, our culture, and its artifacts." The Ute Mountain Tribal Park encompasses lands that contain Native rock art and ancient dwellings. The Southern Ute also host a Bear Dance each spring, as well as a Sun Dance ceremony in the summer. The Bear Dance and the Sun Dance are both important ceremonies that have been practiced among the Ute for hundreds of years.

Still, in the hustle and bustle of modern life, the old ways can get lost. The Ute language has nearly disappeared. Only a handful of adults speak it, and the children are not learning it.

Minority communities often bring their customs to Colorado. This Buddhist stupa is part of the Shambala Mountain Center, which was established by a Tibetan master in 1971.

Minority Communities

According to 2016 estimates from the US Census Bureau, Hispanics account for over 21 percent of

Most Coloradans were not born in the state. Instead, they decided to move to the state for one reason or another. A key driver of this immigration is Colorado's strong economy. Many people relocate to the state because of a job. But there are other reasons that people choose to look for work in Colorado.

The state's weather and its abundant nature are two major reasons people come. It is often said that Denver has three hundred days of sunshine a year—far more than many cities on the East Coast. The mountains are also a short drive from the populated cities of the Front Range. In fact, some cities like Boulder are nestled in the foothills. This means that residents can often walk out their front door and quickly arrive at a trail. This type of lifestyle is very different from that of other American cities like New York City or Washington, DC.

These factors combine to make Colorado an attractive destination for people looking to move. Many people talk about how the typical new residents of Colorado are young, educated, white Americans. They are drawn by the growing tech industry and the promise of an outdoor lifestyle.

However, new residents of Colorado are actually a diverse group of people. The number of Hispanics in the state has been growing in recent years. As of 2016, 21 percent of Coloradans were Hispanic. Around 76 percent of them were born in the United States. The remainder immigrated from Spanish-speaking countries.

In 1870, the percentage of Hispanics in the state was higher than today. It stood at 30 percent. This is not surprising, considering a large part of Colorado used to be part of Mexico. But by 1910, as white settlers flooded into the area, only 3 percent of the state was Hispanic.

The current boom in the Hispanic population can be seen across the state. Many Hispanics call the populous cities of Denver, Fort Collins, and Colorado Springs home. However, the biggest concentration of Hispanics can be seen in the south of the state—near the New Mexico border.

Moving to Colorado

Construction in Denver is evidence of Colorado's strong economy.

Colorado's opportunities for outdoor adventure bring new residents.

The Black American West Museum and Heritage Center is in Denver.

Colorado's population. Hispanics are people whose families come from places such as Mexico, Central America, the Caribbean, South America, or Spain. The majority of Colorado's Hispanics, more than eight hundred thousand, are of Mexican descent.

African Americans make up about 4.5 percent of the population. This is much lower than the national average of 13 percent. Over 3 percent of Coloradans are of Asian descent. This includes Asian Indians, as well as people from China, Japan, Korea, Vietnam, and the Philippines. Between the 2000 and 2010 census, the percentage of African Americans and Asian Americans in the state increased. More people coming to the state led to greater diversity.

Statewide percentages can be misleading, though. They show very little about how people actually live. Minorities are not scattered evenly across the state. Some areas have almost no minority population. Other areas have thriving communities of one or more minority groups.

In Colorado, a variety of programs and organizations are available to help newcomers from foreign nations. Immigrants can find everything from medical and mental health services to English classes, job training, and legal aid. Schools offer special programs for immigrant students and their families. For example, school districts are hiring **bilingual** and multilingual staff members to help parents with questions about their children's education. They are setting up multicultural education programs in schools with large numbers of immigrant children.

FAST FACT

Coloradans have a reputation for being fit. The state's beautiful scenery means many people take up outdoor hobbies like biking and hiking. It's no surprise that Colorado has the lowest adult obesity rate of any state. Colorado's obesity rate was 22.3 percent in 2016. Compare that to the national average of almost 38 percent.

Colorado is known both for its Hispanic food and its delicious peaches. Palisade peaches, grown in the small town of Palisade, are especially famous in the state. You can enjoy a delicious Coloradan dish by making your own peach salsa. Use Palisade peaches if you can. Otherwise, any fresh or even canned peach will do.

Peach Salsa

Ingredients:

- 2 pounds of diced peaches, ideally Palisade peaches
- 1 pound of diced tomatoes
- 1 diced medium red onion
- 1 diced red bell pepper
- 2 tablespoons of lime juice
- 2 teaspoons of salt
- 2 tablespoons of diced fresh cilantro
- Tortilla chips

Palisade peaches are a Colorado favorite.

Directions:

1. Mix the peaches, tomatoes, red onion, and bell pepper together in a bowl.
2. Drizzle the lime juice over the other ingredients.
3. Add the salt.
4. Garnish with fresh cilantro.
5. Serve your salsa with tortilla chips for scooping.

Education

Boulder Valley students work on laptops in this 2014 photo.

Regardless of where they come from or how long they have been living in the state, many Colorado residents see education as an important issue. During local and state elections, citizens often take the politicians' views on education into account when voting. During votes for town or city budgets, many voters are often in favor of giving large amounts of money to the public school system. Coloradans want to ensure that the public schools offer young residents a high level of education, enough teachers, and enough resources.

Bilingual education is a controversial topic in Colorado schools. The idea behind bilingual education seems simple, but there are many viewpoints. Bilingual education allows students who do not speak English to study subjects such as history and science in their native language.

Supporters of bilingual education believe that this is the best option because students do not fall behind in their studies while they are learning English. Opponents believe that bilingual education slows down students' progress in English. They argue that some students will not learn English at all, instead continuing to rely on their native language. The additional expense of hiring bilingual educators is also a concern. Some people believe that the money should be used for resources that all students in the schools could use.

The bilingual education debate is over methods, not goals. Both sides agree that English

Tim Allen

Tim Allen was born in Denver, Colorado, in 1953. He got his start in comedy clubs performing stand-up routines. Later, he began to appear on TV shows. He also does voice acting. He was the voice of Buzz Lightyear in all three *Toy Story* movies.

Melissa Benoist

Benoist was born in Littleton, Colorado. She began acting at a young age and was quickly recognized for her talent. At the age of seventeen, the *Denver Post* included her in a story about successful young actors in the area. She went on to star in numerous TV shows and movies.

Kristen Davis

This Boulder native wanted to be an actress from a young age. She went to college for acting and soon began starring in TV shows. In recent years, she has also become a stage actress. She has performed on Broadway (in New York City), as well as on the West End in London.

Roy Halladay

Halladay was born in Denver. He quickly showed promise in baseball. Soon after he graduated from high school, he was drafted into the minor leagues. Three years later, he entered the majors with the Toronto Blue Jays. He pitched in the majors for the next fifteen years. In 2010, he pitched the twentieth perfect game in Major League Baseball history. Not a single opposing player reached a base. Tragically, Halladay was killed in a one-person plane crash in Florida in 2017.

Celebrities from Colorado

Tim Allen

Melissa Benoist

Roy Halladay

University of
Colorado Boulder

fluency is important. Without it, students have a difficult time attending college and finding jobs. In the past, opponents of bilingual education have proposed laws that would nearly eliminate it in Colorado schools. However, those laws have been defeated. Today, bilingual education programs are on the rise. As of 2015, there were more than one thousand bilingual education programs in the state.

Working Together

Coloradans have diverse political beliefs. Some cities, like Boulder, are among the most liberal in the country. Other cities, like Colorado Springs, are very conservative. Newcomers to Colorado often move to the city that matches their own beliefs. However, the people of Colorado work together to make their state a great place to live despite these differences of opinion.

FAST FACT

Colorado's mountains make it a popular place for rock climbers to live. Large communities of climbers exist in many towns and cities around the state. In fact, you can spot metal rings jutting out of rock faces around Colorado. Climbers fix safety ropes to these rings in case they fall.

Colorado's Biggest Colleges and Universities

(All enrollment numbers are from *US News and World Report* 2018 college rankings.)

1. University of Colorado Boulder

(27,846 undergraduate students)

2. Colorado State University, Fort Collins

(25,177 undergraduate students)

3. Metropolitan State University of Denver

(19,940 undergraduate students)

4. University of Colorado Denver

(14,622 undergraduate students)

5. University of Colorado Colorado Springs

(10,414 undergraduate students)

6. Colorado Mesa University, Grand Junction

(9,595 undergraduate students)

7. University of Northern Colorado, Greeley

(9,503 undergraduate students)

8. Colorado Mountain College, Glenwood Springs

(5,806 undergraduate students)

9. University of Denver

(5,754 undergraduate students)

10. Colorado State University-Pueblo

(5,024 undergraduate students)

University of Colorado Colorado Springs

University of Denver

Colorado State University-Pueblo

Ranching and farming are just two parts of Colorado's robust economy.

4 At Work in Colorado

Colorado has a vibrant economy made up of many different industries. From farming to computer engineering, all sorts of careers are possible in Colorado. As technology changes the nation's economy, Colorado is working hard to stay up to date. At the same time, old industries like farming and manufacturing are still important.

A Changing Economy

Agriculture, mining, and manufacturing are part of what is sometimes called the "old economy." This economy was created by the farm, the mine, and the factory. The "new economy" is created by computers, the internet, and other new technologies.

These new technologies will not replace Colorado's old economy. They will coexist with it. In fact, technology benefits the old economy in many ways. Technology can make operations more efficient and less costly. For example, farmers in eastern Colorado can now computerize their business records, track crop prices and

Windmills and wind turbines harness natural energy.

Peaches grow in a Palisades orchard.

weather systems online, and carry cell phones out to the farthest reaches of their property. Farmers can also use advanced computer systems to map their fields and track the success of crops and irrigation techniques.

Agriculture

Some of Colorado's leading crops are potatoes, onions, and peaches. Agriculture contributes more than $40 billion to the state economy each year.

Some enterprising farmers in Colorado have turned their cornfields into tourist attractions. One of these farmers, Bill English, created a large maze by planting 11 acres (4.5 ha) of corn in the shape of the Colorado state seal. Hundreds of visitors paid admission to try their luck at navigating the twists and turns of this designer cornfield. Other farmers have created corn mazes in different designs for family fun.

In western Colorado, around Grand Junction, farmers grow wine grapes and other fruits such as apples, peaches, apricots, and cherries. These crops are sold throughout the state and to the rest

Cornfields can do more than produce food. Some Colorado farmers have made their fields into corn mazes.

of the country. Some of the produce is packaged or used in food-processing factories in the state.

In both eastern and western Colorado, raising livestock is more widespread than crop farming. The raising of cattle and calves provides more than half of the state's agricultural revenue. Another profitable area for farmers is specialty crops. Small farmers in particular have found that crops such as herbs, ornamental plants, and sod for lawns earn more than traditional field crops such as wheat and corn.

Manufacturing

Manufacturing is the process of taking raw materials (such as cotton) and adding value to them by turning them into finished products (such as cloth). Products manufactured in Colorado include scientific instruments, such as medical devices and electronic equipment, as well as machinery, such as computers and communications equipment. The state also has a large food-processing industry. This includes meat-packing, the production of animal feed,

Mining's Continuing Legacy

Colorado's history is tied to mining. It was the Colorado gold rush that put the state on the map. Thousands of people flooded into Colorado, and cities like Denver sprang up as a result. Soon after, the silver boom drew even more people to the state. Mining jobs provided a steady income to immigrants to Colorado. This rich legacy of mining is still appreciated to this day. There are mining museums in Colorado Springs and Leadville, and in many places around the state you can still try your luck at panning for gold.

This molybdenum mine is located northeast of Leadville.

Today, the mining industry is very different from how it was in the nineteenth century. It is no longer the largest industry in the state. But it is still a thriving, important part of the state's economy. Gold and silver are still mined—in fact, some of the mines sit on the same sites mined more than a century ago. Coal is also mined in Colorado. This source of energy provides the majority of the state's electricity.

In recent years, molybdenum has also been an important metal to Colorado's mining industry. Molybdenum is important because it is used to make steel alloys. Alloys are combinations of two or more metals. They are stronger or more durable than one metal alone. Colorado is the leading state in the country when it comes to producing molybdenum.

As of 2016, more than twenty-five thousand Coloradans are employed in the mining industry. Mining is a vital source of money for the state, as well as an important part of its heritage.

A Vestas plant in Brighton

and brewing. The Coors Brewing Company in Golden, Colorado, has been in operation since 1873. The company employs thousands of people and produces billions of barrels of beer every year.

Colorado is also leading the county in "green" manufacturing. In March 2008, Danish energy company Vestas opened a plant in Windsor, Colorado, that manufactures blades for wind turbines. These modern-day windmills are used to generate electricity. Wind energy is a "clean" energy source.

In 2009, Vestas broke ground on two new factories in Brighton, another blade facility and a nacelle assembly plant. (The nacelle is mounted on the top of the turbine and houses parts including the gearbox, generator, controller, and brake.) The plants employ thousands of people among them. Vestas also built a plant in Pueblo to manufacture the towers for wind turbines. The factory is one of the largest of its kind in the world.

Retail Businesses

Wholesalers are the link between manufacturers who make the merchandise and retailers who sell

FAST FACT

As of 2017, the biggest company in Colorado is Arrow Electronics. It is a Fortune 500 company—meaning it is one of the five hundred largest companies in the United States. Headquartered in Centennial, Colorado, it employs nearly nineteen thousand people worldwide.

Cherry Creek
Shopping Center

to the general public. Wholesalers buy from manufacturers in large quantities and then sell smaller quantities to retailers, who in turn sell the products to regular consumers. About 2.7 percent of Colorado's workforce is employed in wholesale trade, while 11.3 percent work in retail.

The retail industry includes everything from restaurants and bars to supermarkets, department stores, and specialty shops. Day-to-day retail establishments include gas stations, supermarkets, and pharmacies. In addition to these, Denver and other cities have major centers that transform shopping into a recreational activity.

For example, Denver's Cherry Creek neighborhood has tree-lined streets with more than 320 businesses. These include department stores, specialty shops, art galleries, and restaurants. Locals and tourists alike enjoy spending time at Cherry Creek, browsing in shops or eating in the restaurants. Businesses like these help the economy in a few ways. The stores provide a place to sell products manufactured in Colorado. The jobs created by these stores and restaurants keep many Coloradans employed. The taxes that consumers pay when purchasing from these businesses go back to the state.

Providing Services

Denver's Union Station boasts shops, restaurants, and mass transit options.

A service is an activity or process that one person performs for another. It does not transfer ownership of any physical object. A business that rents cars is a service. A business that sells cars is not.

Service industries include everything from banking and insurance to health care, education, transportation, and communications. In addition to these, thousands of providers offer personal and domestic services such as hair styling, child care, and home improvement.

Technology has created many new service jobs. For example, many Coloradans are making a living by programming computers, designing web pages, installing digital television cable, or performing other technical services.

In 1999, the Colorado General Assembly created a new agency: the Governor's Office of Innovation and Technology (OIT). It was renamed the Governor's Office of Information Technology in 2006. The mission of this office is to attract high-technology industries to the state, develop training programs to expand the technology

Inner City Health Center in Denver cares for more than twenty thousand Coloradans each year.

Colorado's Start-Up Scene

Tech start-ups are taking off in Colorado. Start-ups are new businesses looking to grow quickly. They get off the ground with an initial investment of money called **venture capital**. They then hope to make a profit or raise more money before they run out.

The vast majority of venture capital goes to start-ups in Silicon Valley, California. However, Denver and Boulder are becoming more and more important in the world of start-ups. In 2016, Denver start-ups received $380 million in venture capital. This was the fourteenth highest of any American city. Boulder received far less money in total, but much more per person. In fact, Boulder ranked fifth in the amount of venture capital per capita (or per person). For every resident of Boulder, start-ups in the city received $365 in 2016!

Community leaders open the 2017 Denver Startup Week.

Both Denver and Boulder are trying to continue to develop their start-up scene. Each year, both cities have a "Startup Week" that is packed full of events and talks. There is plenty of advice for people looking to start their own company or just find a start-up to work for. Many local start-ups use the week to hire new talent for their company.

There are also many start-up accelerators in Denver and Boulder. These companies—some of which used to be start-ups themselves—help promising start-ups. They find venture capital for great ideas. They also give resources to start-ups to help them grow quickly.

As Colorado's start-up scene keeps growing, more and more tech workers come to the state looking for work. They are drawn not only by jobs but also by the outdoor lifestyle that cities like Boulder promise. This is one aspect of life in Colorado that other up-and-coming start-up cities cannot match.

Great Sand Dunes National Park captivates visitors to Colorado.

workforce, and create a high-speed fiber optic network to streamline government operations.

Tourism in Colorado

Colorado has a thriving tourist industry. There are more than one hundred thousand people working in the tourism industry, which makes it the largest employer in the state. In 2015, tourists spent more than $19 billion in Colorado.

Colorado is known worldwide for its amazing ski slopes.

In winter, people come from all over the world to the state's ski resorts. In summer, they come for camping, river rafting, rock climbing, and many other outdoor activities.

Every year, more than four million people visit Colorado's four national parks: Rocky

The Denver Zoo

Mountain, Mesa Verde, Great Sand Dunes, and Black Canyon of the Gunnison. There, they can experience some of the most incredible natural and cultural wonders the country has to offer, including the highest sand dunes in North America, one of the deepest canyons in the Western Hemisphere, and, of course, the magnificent cliff dwellings of the Ancestral Pueblo people. The state also has forty-two state parks, which provide amazing opportunities for outdoor recreation and adventure.

Many people also visit Colorado for its professional sports teams. The Denver Nuggets are the state's NBA team. Sports Authority Field at Mile High is home to the Denver Broncos football team. Hockey fans attend the games played by the state's NHL team, the Colorado Avalanche. The Colorado Rockies are the state's Major League Baseball team. Denver is the smallest metropolitan area in the United States to have professional teams in all four sports. The

state's economy benefits from the money spent on game tickets and souvenirs.

Conserving the Environment

Environmental protection has long been an important issue for Coloradans. There are laws and programs to preserve open spaces, protect endangered wildlife, and develop clean sources of energy. A group called the Colorado Renewable Energy Society (CRES) develops plans to help conserve energy and use renewable resources such as wind and solar power.

As of 2016, Colorado had more than 1,900 wind turbines that provided 3,026 megawatts of electricity. That is enough to power nearly nine hundred thousand homes. Around 17 percent of Colorado's electricity is provided by wind.

One of the state's most difficult resource management problems is also one of the oldest: water. In this semiarid state, there never seems

Blue Mesa Reservoir is the biggest body of water in Colorado.

to be enough of it, and the distribution is uneven. Most of the state's water comes from the mountains. The state's annual precipitation is generally less than 20 inches (50 cm), with the driest areas receiving only 10 inches (25 cm). In the mountains, the highest elevations may receive as much as 50 inches (125 cm) per year.

Colorado has an advanced system of dams, tunnels, and reservoirs to distribute and conserve water resources. Even with all the planning and technology, droughts are a constant danger. In very dry years, Coloradans may face mandatory water **rationing**.

Coloradans are aware that the unique beauty of their state is good for their economy. It is the foundation for their high quality of life, and the reason that millions of people visit the state each year. Preserving the beauty of the landscape while continuing to develop a variety of industries will be Colorado's challenge for the twenty-first century.

A Strong Economy

The Cheesman Reservoir during a drought in 2002

In 2017, *US News and World Report* ranked Colorado as the state with the best economy in the country. It is a national leader in job growth and low unemployment (the number of people who cannot find work). In August 2017, the unemployment rate in Colorado was just 2.4 percent. That was the second lowest of any state. Compare that to its neighbor New Mexico, which had an unemployment rate of 6.3 percent. As people and businesses continue to move to the state, it is likely that Colorado's economy will remain strong in the future.

Demonstrators gather at Denver's Civic Center Park in 2017.

5 Government

Colorado's state government is similar to the federal—or national—government. There are three branches of government: the executive, legislative, and judicial. Colorado's constitution outlines the different powers these three branches of government have. Since it was first passed in 1876, the constitution has been amended (added to or changed) many times. In fact, it has been amended so many times that there was a recent effort to amend the constitution to make it more difficult to amend.

Branches of Government

Executive

The executive branch consists of the governor, lieutenant governor, and different departments that cover various aspects of public life. The secretary of state, attorney general, and treasurer, as well as the governor and lieutenant governor, are elected by voters. Other department heads are appointed by the governor, with the approval

FAST FACT

Colorado is a swing state. This means that, unlike most states, it is neither firmly Republican nor Democrat. During presidential campaigns, candidates often travel to Colorado to try to change the minds of the people who live there. Local politics are also split. Republicans and Democrats rarely have a solid majority, and they often trade power.

The Governor's Mansion

of the state senate. Elected officials in the executive branch serve four-year terms. They cannot serve more than two terms in a row.

Legislative

Colorado's legislature, or lawmaking body, is called the Colorado General Assembly. It is made up of two houses. The senate has thirty-five members. The house of representatives has sixty-five members. Members of the senate serve four-year terms and cannot hold office for more than two consecutive terms. Members of the house of representatives serve two-year terms and may be elected for up to four terms in a row. Any proposed law must be passed by a majority vote in both houses of the legislature before it goes to the governor for executive approval.

Judicial

The judicial branch enforces the laws of the state. Colorado's court system ranges from municipal (city) and county courts up to the state supreme court. State judges are not elected. They are appointed by the governor. However, during general elections, voters get to decide whether or not to retain the judges. District court judges appear on the ballot every six years. Appeals judges are up for approval every

The Colorado State Capitol opened its doors in 1894.

eight years. Supreme court judges are up every ten years.

Local Government

Colorado's government begins at the local level, with towns, cities, and counties. The governing body of a town is called a board of trustees. The governing body of a city is called a council. Municipal (city and town) governments make ordinances (local laws) covering a variety of local concerns. For example, municipal governments can regulate traffic and parking on city streets. They can also separate business areas from residential areas with zoning ordinances. Cities and larger towns have municipal courts to deal with minor crimes and violations of local laws.

Cities and towns are part of counties. Colorado's sixty-four counties are responsible for carrying out state programs on a local level. Counties are governed by a board of elected commissioners. Other offices within the county include tax assessor, treasurer, and sheriff.

In Colorado, local governments can elect to have home rule, which gives them more control over local matters. Home-rule communities can tailor government policies to their particular needs. They can create their own budget guidelines and zoning regulations. Colorado has close to one hundred cities and towns that are home-rule municipalities. The largest is Colorado Springs.

Federal and statewide laws still apply, which

The Colorado Supreme Court is an important part of the state's judicial branch.

Colorado Springs City Hall

Getting Involved in Politics

It is important to get involved in politics. Politicians are supposed to carry out the will of the people. Even if you're not an adult, you can still contact your representatives and voice your opinion. It is their job to represent everyone in their district.

To find out who your representatives are, you can look on the internet. Your representatives to the US House of Representatives and the US Senate in Washington, DC, can be found at https://www.govtrack.us/congress/members. They represent you when it comes to national issues. Your state representatives can be found at https://leg.colorado.gov/find-my-legislator. They represent you at the statehouse in Denver when it comes to issues in Colorado.

Once you find out who your representatives are, you can find their contact information on their websites. Their websites are linked from the websites above. If you have an opinion you want them to hear, you can write them a letter. Make sure that you write your letter to the correct representative. If it is about a national issue—like health care—write to your representative in Washington, DC. If it is about a local issue, like the environment in Colorado—write to your representative in Denver.

To be polite, address your letter "To the Honorable ____." This shows respect to their position as an elected representative of the people. In your letter, make sure you clearly state your position. Also, be sure to remain respectful. It is much more likely your position will be listened to if you are polite.

places some practical limits on what home-rule communities can do. For example, home-rule communities must budget for state-mandated (that is, state-ordered) programs before they fund their own projects.

Passing New Laws

Sometimes a state resident, official, or **legislator** comes up with an idea for a new state law. The idea is then passed on to a member of the general assembly. The reason is that only a state senator or state representative can officially introduce proposals for new laws. The proposed law is a written document called a bill. A bill can be introduced in either house. The bill is given a number and placed on the schedule of the house that will consider it first. On the appointed day, the bill's sponsor introduces it on the floor.

After this first reading, the bill is assigned to a committee for complete review. Which committee is assigned to analyze a bill depends upon the topic of that bill. For example, a senate bill about water conservation would go to the Committee on Agriculture, Natural Resources, and Energy. A house bill on the same topic would go to the Committee on Agriculture, Livestock, and Natural Resources.

After studying the bill, the committee may postpone it, amend certain parts, or recommend it for passage. Unless a bill is postponed, it will go back to the floor (the entire legislative body) for a second reading. The entire senate or house discusses, debates, and proposes additional amendments to the bill. After this process, they vote. The bill may be accepted as amended, rejected, held over to another day, or sent back to the committee for additional work.

Bills that pass the committee and amendment process go on to yet another reading. After this

Colorado lawmakers at work in 2010

The future home of the National Western Stock Show

NATIONAL WESTERN CENTER

Governor Hickenlooper signs a bill into law.

third reading, there is a final vote. If a bill passes the final vote, it is introduced to the second house. There, the whole process is repeated.

Even when a bill is passed by both houses, the legislators' task may not be done. It often happens that the house and senate adopt different versions of the bill. In these cases, the differences must be fixed before a final version of the bill goes to the governor for his or her signature.

The governor can accept or reject the bill. If the governor signs the bill, it becomes law. If the governor vetoes—or rejects—the bill, it can still pass if two-thirds of both houses vote for the law.

Recent Legislation

In 2016, a constitutional amendment was approved by Colorado voters that raised the minimum wage in the state. Workers must now be paid $9.30 per hour instead of $8.31. This will increase each year until it hits $12 in 2020. The law has a big effect on many people living in Colorado. Other laws are less likely to impact your life. For example, a law passed in 2017 clarifies that it is legal to break a car window to rescue a dog or baby trapped inside.

Glossary

altitude	The height of something in comparison to sea level.
archaeological site	A place where experts dig up artifacts to learn more about history.
bilingual	Relating to two languages; or, in the case of a person, able to speak two languages.
erosion	The process of wind and water wearing away stone and dirt.
federal government	The government that rules over all fifty states. It is made up of the president, Congress, and federal courts like the Supreme Court.
indigenous	Originating in a certain place; the indigenous people of North America are Native Americans.
legislator	Lawmaker; a member of the senate or house at the state or federal level.
mesa	An elevated piece of land with a flat top and a slope down on at least one side.
nomadic	Relating to nomads—people who travel throughout the year as part of their lifestyle.
plateau	A level, flat piece of land that is higher than some neighboring area.
prospector	A person looking to make money by finding minerals or metals like gold.
rationing	Allowing an individual a fixed amount of something in order to conserve it.
suburb	An outlying, residential part of a city.
summit	To "summit" is to reach the top of a mountain.
surveyor	Someone who maps out land.
venture capital	Money given to a start-up so that it can expand.

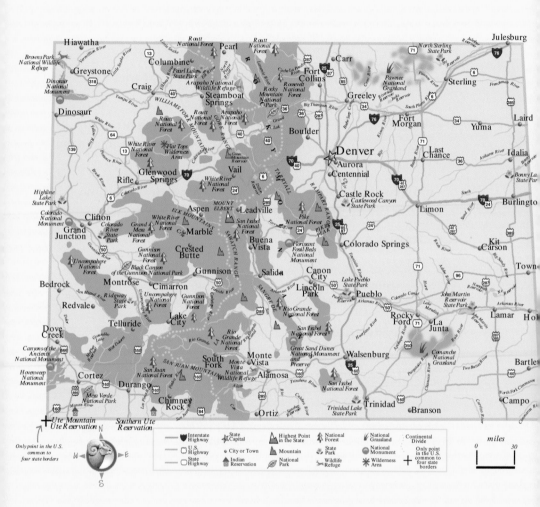

Hiawatha
Browns Park National Wildlife Refuge
Greystone
Dinosaur National Monument
318
Dinosaur
Craig
40
Steamboat Springs
Columbine
13
Pearl Lake State Park
Arapaho National Wildlife Refuge
Pearl
Routt National Forest
Routt National Forest
Rocky Mountain National Park
North Sterling State Park
71
Julesburg
76
Carr
287
25
Fort Collins
85
Greeley
34
Sterling
6
Frenchman River
6
Laird
Yuma
Fort Morgan
34
Laird

White River National Forest
64
139
13
Rifle
6
Glenwood Springs
70
Vail
White River National Forest
Flat Tops Wilderness Area
Arapaho National Forest
36
36
Boulder
76
Fort Morgan

Highline Lake State Park
Colorado National Monument
Clifton
Grand Junction
50
Colorado River State Park
Grand Mesa National Forest
White River National Forest
Aspen
Marble
MOUNT ELBERT
Leadville
San Isabel National Forest
Pike National Forest
Denver
Aurora
Centennial
70
40
287
Castle Rock
Castlewood Canyon State Park
Limon
24
Burlington
Last Chance
36
Idalia
Bonny Lake State Park

Bedrock
Montrose
Uncompahgre National Forest
Ridgway State Park
Cimarron
Gunnison National Forest
Black Canyon of the Gunnison National Park
Crested Butte
Gunnison
50
Buena Vista
Salida
Florissant Fossil Beds National Monument
Colorado Springs
Kit Carson
389
Town
96

Redvale
Telluride
Lake City
Rio Grande National Forest
Canon City
Lincoln Park
Lake Pueblo State Park
Pueblo
John Martin Reservoir State Park
Lamar
Hol

Dove Creek
Canyons of the Ancients National Monument
Hovenweep National Monument
666
550
Rio Grande National Forest
South Fork
Monte Vista
Monte Vista National Wildlife Refuge
Alamosa
Great Sand Dunes National Monument and Preserve
San Isabel National Forest
Walsenburg
25
Rocky Ford
71
La Junta
Comanche National Grassland
Bartle

Cortez
160
666
Mesa Verde National Park
Durango
Chimney Rock
84
Ortiz
Trinidad Lake State Park
Trinidad
160
Branson
Campo

Ute Mountain Ute Reservation
Only point in the U.S. common to four state borders
Southern Ute Reservation
N
W E
S

	Interstate Highway		State Capital		Highest Point in the State		National Forest		National Grassland	Continental Divide
	U.S. Highway		City or Town		Mountain		State Park		National Monument	Only point in the U.S. common to four state borders
	State Highway		Indian Reservation		National Park		Wildlife Refuge		Wilderness Area	

miles
0   30

Colorado State Map and Map Skills

Map Skills

1. What city or town is closest to Colorado's state capital?

2. Which US highway would you take to get from Idalia to Last Chance?

3. What Native American reservation is to the east of the Four Corners (the only point in the US common to four state borders)?

4. Is Pueblo east or west of the Continental Divide?

5. What is the highest point in the state?

6. What is the northernmost city on the map?

7. What point of interest is north of the town of Dinosaur?

8. What interstate runs north to south?

9. What grassland is south of La Junta?

10. What mountains are between Marble and Aspen?

Answers:
1. Aurora
2. US-36
3. Ute Mountain Ute Reservation
4. East
5. Mount Elbert
6. Julesberg
7. Dinosaur National Monument
8. I-25
9. Comanche National Grassland
10. Elk Mountains

More Information

Books

Howell, Brian. *Colorado Rockies.* Minneapolis: ABDO Publishing, 2015.

Laney, Mark. *The Land and Resources of Colorado.* New York: Rosen Publishing, 2015.

Perry, Phyllis J. *Bold Women in Colorado History.* Missoula, MT: Mountain Press Publishing, 2017.

Websites

Colorado Reader
http://mining.state.co.us/SiteCollectionDocuments/Colorado%20Gold%20Rush.pdf
This publication for kids has many stories about mining in Colorado.

Colorado Tourism
http://www.colorado.com
The official website from Colorado's tourism department has information on fun activities and events in the state.

Doing History, Keeping the Past
http://www.unco.edu/hewit/dohist/themes.htm
This website hosted by the University of Northern Colorado and the Colorado Historical Society presents information about Colorado's history for kids.

Rocky Mountain: Suggested Kids' Activities
https://www.nps.gov/romo/planyourvisit/kids.htm
Rocky Mountain National Park's website has a list of suggested activities for kids.

Index

Page numbers in **boldface** are illustrations. Entries in **boldface** are glossary terms.